TABLE OF CONTENTS

INTRODUCTION

The Compassion Capital Fund (CCF), administered by the U.S. Department of Health and Human Services, provided capacity building grants to expand and strengthen the role of nonprofit organizations in their ability to provide social services to low-income individuals. Between 2002 and 2009, CCF awarded 1,277 grants, and the CCF National Resource Center provided training and technical assistance to all CCF grantees. *Strengthening Nonprofits: A Capacity Builder's Resource Library* is born out of the expansive set of resources created by the National Resource Center during that time period, to be shared and to continue the legacy of CCF's capacity building work.

Strengthening Nonprofits: A Capacity Builder's Resource Library contains guidebooks and e-learnings on the following topics:

1. Conducting a Community Assessment
2. Delivering Training and Technical Assistance
3. Designing and Managing a Subaward Program
4. Going Virtual
5. Identifying and Promoting Effective Practices
6. Leading a Nonprofit Organization: Tips and Tools for Executive Directors and Team Leaders
7. Managing Crisis: Risk Management and Crisis Response Planning
8. Managing Public Grants
9. Measuring Outcomes
10. Partnerships: Frameworks for Working Together
11. Sustainability
12. Working with Consultants

Who is the audience for *Strengthening Nonprofits: A Capacity Builder's Resource Library*?

Anyone who is interested in expanding the capacity of nonprofit services in their community – from front–line service providers to executives in large intermediary organizations – will benefit from the information contained in this resource library. The National Resource Center originally developed many of these resources for intermediary organizations, organizations that were granted funds by CCF to build the capacity of the faith-based and community-based organizations (FBCOs) they served. As such, the majority of the resources in *Strengthening Nonprofits: A Capacity Builder's Resource Library* support intermediary organizations in their capacity building efforts. However, funders of capacity building programs (Federal program offices and foundations) and the nonprofit community (including FBCOs) at large will also find these resources helpful. In addition, individuals working to build capacity within a program or an organization will be able to use these resources to support their efforts to implement change and make improvements.

The ***Partnerships: Framework for Working Together*** guidebook will be helpful to any organization or coalition of organizations that wants to know more about establishing and managing partnerships.

Who developed the ***Partnerships: Framework for Working Together*** guidebook?

The guidebook was originally developed by CCF National Resource Center with assistance from Mark Publow. It was updated in 2010 for the Department of Health and Human Services by the National Resource Center.

OVERVIEW

As pressures on faith-based and community organizations (FBCOs) increase and the issues we face become more complex, the idea of partnerships can hold much promise. Through partnerships we can contribute our small part and reap the benefits of everyone's effort; we can accelerate learning and distribute skills and knowledge; and we can add depth and breadth to our community impact. To make real the promise of partnerships, however, we must be prepared to build, sustain, and evaluate them in a thoughtful way.

This guidebook will help organizations answer several key questions:

- Why are effective partnerships important?
- What are the different forms that partnerships can take?
- What are key steps to establishing effective partnerships?
- What are key steps to managing effective partnerships in order to achieve mutually agreed-upon outcomes?

Why Form Partnerships?

While there are many nationally recognized benefits and advantages to partnership development, the answer to why one seeks to establish partnerships is relatively simple. There is added value in working with other organizations.

The benefits of effective partnerships do not appear overnight. Establishing effective and inclusive partnerships takes time, and it is important for you to create the right framework from the start and review the structure and process of the partnership on an ongoing basis to measure its success or failure.

What Is a Partnership?

A working definition of a partnership is "a collaborative relationship between entities to work toward shared objectives through a mutually agreed division of labor."[1]

While this working definition is not very precise, it does help distinguish partnerships from other forms of aid relationships. Partnerships are inherently complex vehicles for the delivery of practical solutions on the ground and at the strategic level. Several studies of how partnerships operate indicate that practitioners manage the complexity by adopting a long-term, flexible, and organic approach. Why organic? During the course of these partnerships, organizations often evolve as they learn more about effective management, build capacity, and gain valuable experiences. In that sense, partnerships act as learning mechanisms that teach you to be better at what you do and enable you to achieve your goals.

If you are considering a potential partnership, you should become familiar with several key components of the most common approaches to partnerships:

Leadership

Partnerships imply a shared leadership among respected individuals who are recognized and empowered by their own organizations and trusted by partners to build consensus and resolve conflicts.

---

1   World Bank, Partnerships Group, Strategy and Resource Management, "Partnership for Development: Proposed Actions for the World Bank" (discussion paper, May 20, 1998), p. 5.

Common Understanding

A common understanding of the framework, culture, values, and approach of partner organizations needs to exist. Also important is a clear understanding of individual members' roles and responsibilities regarding the division of labor.

Purpose

A shared common vision and purpose that builds trust and openness and recognizes the value and contribution of all members also needs to exist. Additionally, shared and transparent decision-making processes—extending the scope of influence over and involvement with other services and activities—will prove essential to your partnership. Shared goals and aims, understood and accepted as being important by each partner, lead to improved coordination of policies, programs, and service delivery, and, ultimately, better outcomes.

Culture and Values

Shared can-do values, understanding, and an acceptance of differences (e.g., values, ways of working) are all key components of a successful partnership. Having respect for the contributions of all partners, combined with an absence of status barriers, will lead to the active involvement of members who are identified as being effective, representative, and capable of playing a valued role in the partnership.

Learning and Development

A healthy partnership promotes an atmosphere of learning. This may involve monitoring and evaluation aimed at improving members' performance. Investing in partner skills, knowledge, and competence needs to be highly valued within the partnership. This open mindset and spirit of facilitation creates opportunities to shape each other's work and learn together. In this environment, members can more effectively reflect on both developmental successes and failures.

Communication

If a partnership is going to succeed in the area of communication, strong feedback loops are required. Effective communication at all levels within the partnership and within partner organizations, sharing and accessing all knowledge and information, needs to exist.

Performance Management

Management practices and resources are required to achieve the partnership goals and complement the intended purpose of the partnership. Specifically, members must demonstrate accountability for the actions they take and ownership of delivery of the objectives and targets for which they are responsible.

You must remain equally aware of key barriers to a working relationship with a potential partner. Furthermore, as relationships evolve, partners must work to resolve any barriers. Below is a list of potential barriers to successful partnerships for you to consider.

BARRIERS TO SUCCESSFUL PARTNERSHIPS

- Limited vision/failure to inspire
- One partner manipulates or dominates, or partners compete for the lead
- Lack of clear purpose and inconsistent level of understanding purpose
- Lack of understanding roles/responsibilities
- Lack of support from partner organizations with ultimate decision-making power
- Differences of philosophies and manners of working
- Lack of commitment; unwilling participants
- Unequal and/or unacceptable balance of power and control
- Key interests and/or people missing from the partnership
- Hidden agendas
- Failure to communicate
- Lack of evaluation or monitoring systems
- Failure to learn
- Financial and time commitments outweigh potential benefits
- Too little time for effective consultation

Key Components of Partnership Development

As opportunities arise, organizations need practical advice on whether or not to form strategic partnerships. Research and practitioner evidence suggests the following overarching principles of good practice with regard to partnership development, as well as specific issues you need to consider when evaluating the structure of a partnership. You may have questions ranging from "Who should be involved in this partnership?" to "How will each member operate?" Some common themes among these critical success factors include:

- Balancing requirements and flexibility within the structure and operation of the partnership

- Developing a stable foundation for the membership, rationale, and activities of the partnership while allowing sufficient flexibility for these components to develop and evolve in response to external and internal demands

- Understanding that partnerships go through a life cycle of development, from initial set-up stages through full-scale implementation to maturity

It is important to note that these principles can be applied across different levels and functions of partnership arrangements. However, existing partnerships or those organizations seeking to set up a partnership, should apply all of these principles, as they set the standards for partnership development as described in this guidebook. Following these standards will ensure that partnerships are working effectively and will successfully enable them to achieve their overall goals.

The first step in evaluating a potential partnership is to recognize and agree upon the need. A common approach in making this decision requires that you:

- Identify principal desired partnership achievements.

- Identify the factors associated with successful partnership development.

- Identify any principal barriers to the partnership.

- Acknowledge and recognize the extent of dependency upon individuals to achieve goals.

- Focus on partnership added value (Ask yourself, "How can we achieve more or better results through collaboration?")

In a later section, this guidebook further addresses how to determine the need for a partnership. Once you have determined the need exists, you will want to consider the following fundamental principles and standards for partnership development:

Emphasize clarity of leadership

Whoever leads the development of the partnership needs to be recognized and empowered by his/her own organization and trusted by the partners.

Provide clarity in understanding

Framework, culture, values, and the approach of partner organizations will in many cases need to be the subject of explicit discussion. Partners need to be clear about and understand their roles and responsibilities, defining who does what regarding delivery of activities of the partnership.

Recognize and allow the differences in culture/practice that exist among partners

Do not adopt an approach that suppresses different cultures and practices, as it will lead to conflict. Recognize and accept that others have a diversity of skills and innovative abilities. For example, only address significant differences if the lack of coordination of different planning and decision-making processes within partner organizations prevents implementation of partnership strategies/activities.

Ensure clarity of purpose

- Ensure the partnership is built on a shared and common vision, and mutually agreeable service principles.

- Ensure that all partners understand and agree on the purpose and outcome of the partnership. In other words, everyone must have a shared vision regarding why the partnership was developed and what it hopes to achieve. This will help build a common purpose and shared commitment.

- Develop a shared decision-making process in which partners have equal power. Decisions should not be the result of consensus based on the lowest common denominator.

- Define clear partnership aims and objectives, with objectives expressed as outcomes for users.

- Ensure that partnership aims and objectives are realistic.

- Publicize agreed-upon and understood common aims and priorities.

- Acknowledge the existence of separate organizational aims and objectives and their connection to jointly agreed aims and objectives.

Ensure a level of ownership and management commitment

This commitment is required from the senior level in all partner organizations (e.g., directors, members, and trustees). Make sure the commitments are expressed through practical support for the partnership in terms of resources and cost implications. Do this as soon as the partnership is operational. You will also want to:

- Agree to the appropriate/relevant partners

- Secure widespread ownership within and outside of partner organizations

- Recognize and nurture individuals with networking skills

- Cascade decisions and encourage contacts/networks across partner organizations at intermediate and front-line staff levels

Develop and maintain trust

Fairness involves the conduct of the partnership, affording equal status among the partners and equality regarding the distribution of partnership benefits or gains. You will also want to:

- Ensure that the partnership is able to sustain a level of trust when faced with external problems that inhibit the contribution of individual partners

- Ensure that the right people are in the right place at the right time

- Ensure that the trust that is built up within partnerships is protected from any mistrust that develops in parent organizations

Finally, be open and honest, and communicative. Exchanging information in an open network will help build shared understanding and values. The need for effective communication goes beyond the partnership itself.

Develop clear partnership working arrangements

An effective partnership's working arrangements result in a clear outcome and maintain value for the contribution of all partners, avoiding domination of particular members and/or organizations. The partnership must emphasize clarity of roles and responsibilities while valuing the separate roles and the different experience and skill levels required. You will also want to:

- Ensure transparency and awareness in the financial and non-monetary resources each partner brings to the partnership.

- Distinguish between single and joint responsibilities and accountabilities.

- Ensure that the prime focus is on process and outcomes, not structure and inputs.

Finally, following an agreement by the partners, ensure that the purpose, role, responsibility of members, main aims, objectives, and outcomes for the partnership are documented within whatever medium the partnership requires, e.g., business plan, terms of reference, or constitution.

Account for performance management

All partners ought to agree at the outset regarding how they are to measure their success and how they are to incorporate the measurements into the best value requirements for continuous improvement. This measurement process must include arrangements for monitoring and reviewing how effectively the partnership itself is working. Additionally, you will want to consider and resolve outstanding accountability and governance issues.

Recognize the opportunity for learning experiences and sharing good practices

Remember, a partnership can be considered a work in progress. This means that you will want to agree to a range of success criteria regarding your partnership. Additionally, you will want to:

- Ensure that feedback flows to and from parent organizations.

- Celebrate and publicize local success and root out continuing barriers.

- Reconsider and revise partnership aims, objectives, and arrangements.

Categories of Partnerships

Considerations in any partnership will vary based on the kinds of organizations involved, as well as on the intensity and interdependence of the relationship you choose to have. Following are some categories of partnerships that will help you determine what kind of working and management relationship works best given your specific situation.

BASICS OF PARTNERSHIP DEVELOPMENT
- ☐ Need for Partnership
- ☐ Clarity of Leadership
- ☐ Clarity of Understanding
- ☐ Different cultures/practices
- ☐ Clear Purpose
- ☐ High Commitment Levels
- ☐ Trust
- ☐ Clear Working Arrangements
- ☐ Performance Management Systems
- ☐ Learning/Exchanges of Good Practices

The key for you to establish and maintain successful partnerships is to find a way to build on the strengths of all partners in various categories. In recent years, there has been a significant increase in the number of institutional "sponsors" of partnerships focusing on community improvement. Agencies at the Federal and state levels, universities, corporations, and national nonprofits have all provided support to partnerships with community impacts. Some of the most common categories of partnership are listed below.

Partnerships among Community-based Nonprofit Service Organizations

From a community development perspective, the test to determine if these partnerships are effective is whether they actually contribute to what will empower people for social and economic change.[2] Organizations linking community and institutional interests list the following components regarding the share of work: close, mutual cooperation; common goals; shared involvement in decision making; sharing risks and benefits; common interests; responsibilities; and power. These components focus on both the process of the partnership (e.g., shared decision making, shared power) and the capacity of each partner to assume responsibility for a share of the work.

Capacity of Partnerships

A growing body of research calls attention to the role of social capital, or community social capacity, as the source of the ability to identify problems and needs, achieve a workable consensus on goals and priorities, and work in partnership with other organizations to achieve goals.[3] One framework regarding "Theories of Neighborhood Change" suggests four fundamental characteristics of community capacity:[4]

- A sense of community, portraying a degree of connectedness among members

- A level of commitment, investing time and energy in community well-being, often funneled into local organizations

- Mechanisms for problem solving, addressing issues, and taking collective action with external organizations

- Access to resources (human and financial) through commitments of institutional partners

In the context of partnerships, without community capacity, neighborhoods are at risk of being merely the recipient of goods or services, rather than a true partner in local revitalization efforts. In addition to levels of social or community capacity, in order to function as a partner, each organization must have a degree of organizational capacity to manage projects and budgets and establish manageable objectives to keep people involved.

In other words, if only one side of the partnership is involved in actual project management, there is no assurance that it is representative of shared interests or that there is any capacity for sustainability.

Process of Partnerships

Along with the individual capacity of each partner, it is important to examine the *process* of the actual partnership. There are a number of properties to assess when considering how the "community" and the "partnership" establish and sustain a relationship. The locus of control for these properties is critical to the sustainability of the partnership and the community development initiative.

Consider the following four categories of properties that are important in a community partnership:

1. **Leadership** – There are many styles of leadership in both formal and informal organizational structures. The key is noting *who* is providing the leadership in the partnership.

---

2   Kilpatrick, Sue, Susan Johns, Bill Mulford, Ian Falk, and Libby Prescott. "More than an Education: Leadership for Rural School-Community Partnerships," Barton, ACT: Rural Industries Research and Development Corporation, 2002.

3   Mattessich, Paul W. and Barbara Monsey. *Community Building: What Makes It Work.* St. Paul, MN: Amherst H. Wilder Foundation, 1997.

4   Chaskin, Robert J. and Prudence Brown. "Theories of neighborhood change," in *Core Issues in Comprehensive Community-Building Initiatives.* Rebecca Stone, ed. Chicago, IL: Chapin Hall Center for Children at the University of Chicago, 1996.

2. **Primary funding** – An institutional partner can bring resources to the table and limit discussion to those resources or bring linkage to resources, or there can be a cooperative effort to secure unattached resources.

3. **Goals** – Goals can be set in the absence of resources. You can develop them through consensus decision-making or they can be accepted because one party in the discussion is the "expert."

4. **Process** – Decision processes in community organizations and community institutions can be either inclusive or exclusive. Important to community development is how actively, and deeply, the community was engaged.

Cross-sector Partnerships

Cross-sector partnerships are between organizations from different fields: non-profits, business, government, and academic. These partnerships can be challenging to maintain over time because you often have divergent needs and cultures. However, within cross-sector partnerships this weakness can be turned into a strength. The key is to find common ground and purpose that everyone in the partnership has a stake in.

Benefits to Partners

Why should potential partners participate in a cross-sector relationship? What benefits will result in their favor? The answers lie in the very nature of FBCOs; they are connected to the community and are able to build infrastructures that can create long-term capacity. They are more representative of community concerns.[5] And while FBCOs are often required to provide certain geographic connections in order to maintain funding, other types of organizations are not required to do so and can therefore enable access to greater funding resources.

Moreover, this type of cross-sector partnership provides FBCOs with greater citywide/region-wide connections and provides the other organizations with greater grassroots connections. Another benefit for governmental/business/academic organizations is the positive public perception regarding the interest and commitment to the community and its development. These organizations also benefit from being able to participate in community development without having to deal with political and legal regulations, permit issues, etc. The result of a cross-sector partnership is a win-win situation for all the parties involved.

Partnerships between Donors and Recipients

Partnerships between donors and recipients can often create confusion. Is a partnership just receiving money? In order to answer similar questions, partnerships may be better understood by identifying what they are not:

A partnership is not a gift. A partnership aims at taking advantage of what the recipient, as well as the donor, can bring to the relationship. This can include local expertise, on-site workers, and a better understanding of priorities, needs, and constraints. Even more important, a partnership seeks joint "ownership" of the relationship and tries to build the capacity of the recipient to undertake sustainable development.

A partnership is not a relationship based on "if…then" terms. This means that donors cannot impose conditions to coerce FBCOs to do things that they don't want to do in order to obtain resources they need. A partnership recognizes that both sides must be involved in defining the terms of the relationship.

---

5   Chaskin, Robert J. and Prudence Brown. "Theories of neighborhood change," in *Core Issues in Comprehensive Community-Building Initiatives*. Rebecca Stone, ed. Chicago, IL: Chapin Hall Center for Children at the University of Chicago, 1996.

Baum, Howell S. *The Organization of Hope: Communities Planning Themselves.* Albany, NY: State University of New York, 1997.

A partnership is not a principal-agent relationship between a donor and a recipient. In a partnership, the donor cannot prescribe the terms of the relationship in the way that an employer can specify terms of employment when hiring a worker.

A partnership is not simply a "team" activity. In an ideal sports team, everyone has exactly the same interest in winning, and the team members win or lose together. While the members of a partnership development certainly have strong interests in common, they are likely to have some divergent interests too.

Finally, although the formal terms of a partnership may be expressed in a valid contract under international law, the donor and recipient usually have no intention of using courts to resolve their conflicts. Instead, like nations bound by treaties, partners rely mainly on each other's need to maintain a good reputation to secure future agreements.

Additional Types of Partnerships

Some other specific types of partnerships are also available for your consideration. Within the description of each type are examples of how the partnership might be expressed under typical circumstances.

Collaboration

Characteristics: Greater autonomy, no permanent organizational commitment

Example: Organizational partnerships:

- Sharing information
- Coordinating efforts
- Not including shared, transferred, or combined services, governance, resources, or programs
- Having no integration

Strategic Alliance

Characteristics: Decision-making power is shared or transferred

Examples: Joint programming:

- Management of a program of mutual interest to participating organizations' missions
- Administrative consolidation:
- Being agreement-driven
- Ongoing partnerships involving joint management of one or more functions, e.g., administrative or program-related
- Partners still operate independently

Integration

Characteristics: Involves changes to structure and control

Examples: Management service organizations:

- Established to provide some or all administrative functions, e.g., fundraising, accounting functions

  Joint ventures:

  » Two or more organizations creating a new structure to advance an administrative or program-related function

Parent-subsidiaries:

» One organization—either new or a designated organization—overseeing functions of another

Mergers:

» Previously separate organizations completely combining program, administrative, and governance functions[6]

Funding Alliances Established to Provide or Share Funds

- Separate organizations come together in a recipient-donor relationship or share a larger grant/donation

- Issues of fiscal and administrative management can be a great hindrance

- In order to mitigate issues, a separate body can be created to manage the funds and allocate them to each partner organization as determined in the original agreement

Cost-sharing/Grant-match Partnerships

- Cost-sharing occurs when one organization provides certain resources and the other organization provides different resources, e.g., the universities provide the facilities, faculty, and the new environment in which the Federal government selectively invests

- Grant-match occurs when one organization provides a grant and the recipient provides a match in services, cash, maintenance, voluntary effort, or supplies

- Both partners share the benefits; both share the costs[7]

FORMING PARTNERSHIPS

Now that you hopefully have a better understanding of the key components and categories of partnerships, how should you begin the process of partnership development? There are three essential steps to making sure you get your partnership off to a successful start:

1. Defining the need for a partnership
2. Starting the process
3. Setting up and maintaining the partnership

Step One: Defining the Need for a Partnership

The goal of partnerships is to achieve more than individual organizations can achieve on their own. In other words, the whole of the partnership adds more than the sum of the individual parts. Bear in mind that the partnership should not be the end in and of itself but a means to an end. Therefore, establishing a partnership may not always be the most appropriate decision.

---

6 Connolly, Paul and Peter York. *Pulling Together: Strengthening the Nonprofit Sector through Strategic Restructuring.* New York, NY: TCC Group, 2002.

7 The Association of American Universities, Council of Governmental Relations, National Association of State Universities and Land-Grant Colleges, and Federal Demonstration Partnership, "Cost Sharing," (comments on a report from the National Science and Technology Council, 1999). Available online at http://www.stanford.edu/dept/DoR/PIship/cs_paper.html.

Identifying Self-Interest

In defining the need for a partnership, you should think not only about what the partnership can accomplish as a whole, but about the potential concrete benefits to your organization in particular. Each potential partner should answer the following questions and discuss their answers with one another:

- *Short-term interest*: What does your organization need to get in the next twelve months to stay engaged in the partnership?

- *Long-term interest*: What does your organization need to get in the next eighteen to thirty-six months to stay engaged in the partnership?

Possible answers might include additional organizational members or volunteers; enhanced products or services; greater community credibility or support; and improved access to businesses, agencies, or foundations.

In addition to this exercise and dialogue, the following questions provide a checklist for testing out whether forming a partnership is the appropriate choice.

CHECKLIST FOR EVALUATING POTENTIAL PARTNERSHIPS

☐ **Is there a need for a partnership?**

On what basis is the partnership being set up? Is there a group of like-minded people with a shared vision who have decided that developing a partnership is the only route to achieving a goal? Are potential partners willing to support this?

☐ **What organizational and collective benefits will be gained from setting up this partnership arrangement?**

Are there clearly identified goals that only a partnership arrangement could help achieve? What is the "added value" for potential partners? What is your – and their – organizational self-interest? Are they willing to sign up to this? What exactly is the partnership trying to achieve? How will involving others help the partnership to achieve its goals?

Note the benefits and goals below and test with potential partners:

☐ **Is someone else already doing something similar?**

Do other organizations have similar or the same goals? If so, have you considered approaching them to become part of their partnership arrangement to ensure work is not being duplicated? If this is not appropriate or feasible, think about incorporating lessons they have learned into the new partnership arrangements.

Note your research conducted on potential duplicate partnerships:

☐ **Is there a commitment from partner organizations to support the partnership?**

Have you approached partner organizations with the possibility of setting up a partnership? Was their response positive? Was such a proposal supported at a high level and a clear commitment given to this? (It is important that partner agencies understand and agree to such proposals in order to support and direct future decision-making processes.)

Note the outcome of any work carried out to identify potential commitments from partner organizations:

Step Two: Starting the Process

Partnerships have to be developed and nurtured in a manner that respects and recognizes each individual. Picture a group working as a team that ultimately wants to achieve the same goal no matter how or what it takes to achieve it. The process for building and developing relationships within the partnership is not just the responsibility of the person(s) who lead the group, but of everyone in that group.

The stages of developing a partnership could be based on the four stages of project management team building—forming, storming, norming, and performing. *Forming* the group by bringing people together is part of the initial stages of the process of building the partnership. The next stage, after the group has met on two or three occasions, is when people start questioning the purpose of the partnership (i.e., "Why am I here and what is my role?"). It is important to work through this stage of *storming* in order for the group to be open and honest about what their perceptions are regarding the various definitions of the overall goal/vision. *Norming*, the stage where the partnership is reaching shared agreements, and *performing* are discussed later in this guidebook.

It is also important during the initial stages to agree on a set of ground rules for the partnership. This may seem obvious, but very few groups perform this fundamental requirement necessary for valuing and respecting the individual partners.

☐ **Identify responsibilities, arrangements, and objectives of leadership:**

Who will take the lead? Who will have responsibility for driving the partnership agenda forward? Is there a clear written statement of the partnership leader's objectives and responsibilities? What accountability arrangements are in place? Do all members agree to these procedures? You will want to devise a clear written statement of who will take the lead/joint lead, their main objectives and responsibilities, and to whom they will be accountable.

Document how you will obtain member agreement on these procedures:

☐ **Identify the shared vision and goals:**

Is there a genuine shared vision and set of goals across the partnership? Is there a common understanding of and agreement to the vision and objectives, and are these documented? Do all partners understand how to achieve this? It is important that members are clear about the purpose and ultimate goal of the partnership.

Document the shared vision and goals:

☐ **Determine plans and priorities:**

Does the partnership have a strategy/action plan that clearly sets out why the partnership was set up, what it is going to achieve, who is going to do what, and by when? Where does this strategy/plan fit into wider strategies, and how does it link into partner strategies/local priorities? The partnership needs to have a strategy and action plan that sets out a clear structure. The strategy needs to reflect how the partnership will manage change and evaluate how well it is doing.

Document the partnership plan, priorities, and links to other relevant strategies/plans:

☐ **Determine the function and nature of the partnership:**

What is the nature of the partnership? Has this been established? It is important that members of the partnership are clear at what level and function this partnership is operating (e.g., advisory, strategic, networking, joint working, or project-based).

Document what members agree is the function and nature of the partnership:

☐ **Identify benefits for target groups:**

What are the benefits to target groups in establishing this partnership? Has the partnership agreed or identified outcomes for specific target groups? If not, why not? This is relevant when the partnership is setting outcome measures. Benefits to target groups need to be clearly established and agreed upon by partners.

Benefits for target groups include:

Outcomes include:

TIPS FOR STARTING THE PROCESS

✓ Ensure members of the partnership participate from the earliest opportunity to help determine the entity's structure, process, and priorities

✓ Ensure aims and objectives are clear at the outset and that they link to targets/strategy of partner organizations and the main body of accountability

Step Three: Setting Up and Maintaining the Partnership

Research suggests that there can often be ambiguity (or even conflict) regarding the division of responsibility between a partnership and the individual partners. The distinction between strategic and operational decision making is often the most difficult to resolve, with a reluctance by key partners to delegate authority to the partnership. Clear procedures are needed for everyone to understand how agreements on action will be taken and to help create a sense of shared responsibility for achievements and failures of the partnership.

These procedures should be agreed upon in writing, setting out the key aims, objectives, and outcomes of the partnership. These documents could take the form of a legal constitution or contract (sometimes referred to as "terms of reference"). It is also essential that any document reflects the business plan or strategy that forms the basis of the partnership's work. This will give the partnership structure and boundaries to work within, allowing flexibility to change and grow.

Keep in mind that the partnership needs to constantly review its purpose, goals, and targets. In order for members of the group to have an idea of what they are meant to do, an agreed-upon work program/action plan must be promulgated. Again, the *storming* stage discussed in Step Two leads to the next stage in the partnership, *norming*. Here, the group will be reaching shared agreements, developing protocols, delivering synergetic responses, and avoiding duplication. Otherwise, after the initial *forming* and *storming* stages, the group could reach a level of frustration and stagnation, leading the group to fail.

The group needs to take time out to answer the following questions, which could form the basis of a terms of reference or partnership agreement.

CHECKLIST FOR SETTING UP AND MAINTAINING THE PARTNERSHIP

☐ **Is there a genuine shared vision and set of goals across the partnership?**

A common understanding of, and agreement to, the vision and objectives needs to be reflected in any project brief, business plan, terms of reference, and/or work program.

Document the vision and agreed goals:

☐ **Are there clearly identified aims that all partners can articulate and agree to?**

The partnership's aims and goals need to be reflected in its actions and practices.

Document accepted aims:

☐ **Is the purpose of the partnership clear? Are the members clear on what their role and responsibilities are? Are members clear on the "added value" of the partnership?**

Members need to agree and understand what their role and responsibilities are within the context of the purpose and outcomes of the partnership. Members need to understand their role in collective decision-making, delivering activities, and representing the partnership.

Document roles and responsibilities of members:

☐ **What skills and competencies do we need to manage and support the partnership? Has a full assessment been made of the skill and competencies required to support/manage the partnership?**

The partnership needs to understand what skills and competencies it will need to achieve the agreed goals, as well as to ensure processes are effective. Consideration will need to be given to making training resources available.

Document skills and competencies:

☐ **To whom will the partnership report? Is there a process to report on progress?**

Document the lines of accountability/reporting processes:

☐ **Is there an accepted process for decision-making? Who is the accountable individual for the partnership?**

The decision-making process needs to be understood by all members of the partnership. Decisions should be made through recognized processes with partners having equal power. Processes for decision-making need to define a quorum, how decisions will be recorded, and arbitration processes.

Document processes for decision-making:

☐ **Is there an accepted performance management framework? Are processes in place to monitor performance and act on results? Do defined criteria exist against which to benchmark achievements?**

Individuals responsible for delivery of the plan to the partnership need to be specified.

Document the performance management framework:

Document the criteria to benchmark achievements:

☐ **Is there an accepted commitment to joint investments/resources to support the partnership by all the organizations/individuals?**

Resources mean more than just money; they include time, knowledge, energy, and personnel.

Document the accepted commitment to joint investment/resources:

☐ **Is there a robust communication strategy in place? Do partners know about each others' organizations and what the pressures and imperatives are? Do partners talk to each other about their organizations agendas and priorities?**

It is important to have an effective communication system in place at all levels within the partnership and within partner organizations, sharing knowledge and information.

Document the communication strategy:

☐ **Are there accepted ground rules for partnership work that include the reconciliation of different organizational cultures and ways of working?**

Being open and honest, communicating, and exchanging information in open networks will also help to build trust within the partnership.

Document accepted ground rules:

❑ **Is there an accepted program for partners to invest time so they can identify and agree to the vision, goals, and targets?**

It is important at the initial stages of setting up the partnerships that members agree on the vision, goals, and targets. The requirement for and stated outcomes of "away days" need to be documented in Terms of Reference or partnership agreements. It is important to repeat this exercise to review these goals and targets, checking that they are on track.

Document the process established to agree on vision, goals and targets, and how these will be monitored and evaluated:

❑ **Is there a clear, measurable plan for administering the partnership? Is the plan clearly linked to partnership aims and objectives, and do all parties agree to this plan?**

Any partnership needs to have structure and processes so members clearly understand its purpose, aims, objectives, and outcomes. The plan should also indentify the process to review/update aims and outcomes when monitoring reveals it is out of date or reflects changing circumstances.

Document the administration plan:

❑ **Are there clear processes in place to ensure all new members of the partnership are well informed of its purpose, aims, and objectives?**

As the partnership grows and existing members leave, new members will come on board. It is important that each new member has a clear understanding of the purpose of the partnership. Spend time to induct new members into understanding and supporting the partnership's aims.

Document the "orientation processes" utilized for new members:

TIPS FOR SETTING UP AND MAINTAINING THE PARTNERSHIP

✓ Agree on the structure, process, and support mechanisms for the partnership

✓ Agree on the main purpose/priorities

✓ Agree on the performance management process

✓ Identify a work program

Case Study: Setting Up and Maintaining a Successful Partnership

The Duluth Area Family YMCA and United Way of Greater Duluth, as partners, managed two projects funded by the U.S. Department of Health and Human Services' Administration for Children and Families. Duluth YMCA and United Way worked together so seamlessly that it seemed like they were intertwined. The program manager for training and technical assistance was technically employed by the YMCA, being supervised by Duluth YMCA's senior program director, but worked at the United Way offices down the street.

How can that possibly work? Here are notes from an interview with Duluth YMCA senior program director Blair Gagne and United Way of Greater Duluth president Paula Reed designed to capture their wisdom and insight into partnership management.

Open Communication

"There is a need for open and constant communication to ensure that everything flows accordingly," said Paula.

This means that all parties need to be open and willing to communicate honestly with one another. In talking about addressing barriers, Paula and Blair both quickly responded that open and honest communication is the key to working through challenging situations. They each recounted a situation to demonstrate:

Situation #1 – There was a staffing issue in the partnership, and a quick solution was needed. Rather than making a decision at the top of the organization, the team brought all affected staff persons from both organizations to the table and had an open, honest conversation about the options and the consequences of those options.

"All key peopled were involved in addressing our staffing issue, even though it was occurring in United Way's office," said Paula. "We made the effort to ensure that we were *all* on the same page and aware of the circumstances before a final decision was made. Open communication has been critical in building the strong relationships that we have, and it is clear that the 'team approach' is working very well for us."

Situation #2 – A consultant was brought in to help with a situation without all parties being involved. There were concerns about the use of a consultant which, left unsaid, could slowly erode the trust that existed between the two organizations. In this situation, the concern was brought up at the first opportunity.

"This open discussion even helped strengthen the relationship," said Blair. "In some ways, a collaboration is like a marriage – things don't always go as planned, and saying sorry and moving on is part of a healthy relationship."

Develop Relationships

"Developing relationships within all levels of a partnership/collaboration is the most important element of a successful partnership," said Blair.

He added that it is equally important to complement the professional relationship with a personal one: "In all the collaborations/partnerships/coalitions I have been involved in, the time spent in getting to know each other has been our best investment. Whether it is going out to lunch together, meeting after work, golfing, or attending different program events, this time is critical."

Define the Partnership

Key to developing the relationship, according to Blair, is defining the partnership. All parties should understand the nature of the relationship and how decisions will be made.

"There is a difference in the terms 'partnership,' 'coalition,' and 'collaboration'," said Blair. "Know them up front."

During their regular leadership team meetings, Blair and Paula implement consensus decision making.

"We defined what this meant and discussed examples of how decisions would be made," added Blair, noting that the extra effort to define the partnership at the beginning eases future conflicts and roadblocks.

Work Together for the Good of the Community

"Both parties have to be fully committed to working with each other and sharing decision-making responsibilities," said Paula.

Within a partnership or coalition, according to Paula, the public good needs to be the ultimate factor when making decisions: "In a partnership, goals are not necessarily intended to meet the needs of one side or the other. Rather, whatever the partnership is working towards becomes front and center. Decisions are made based on what is best for the overall situation, not just one partner."

"It is important for the person spearheading the relationship to let go of turf issues," added Blair. "This modeling can help people realize that we need to do what is best for the *community*, and not just *me*. Lead organizations that quibble about every little thing are setting up a scenario of failure."

A Perfect Pair

It is apparent that Blair and Paula have fun together, laughing at themselves and each other throughout the process. They are filled with advice for establishing good relationships.

"When I don't understand something, I ask questions until I do," said Paula. "Make extra effort to be inclusive, even if it takes a bit more time and energy. While it takes more time to ensure that everyone has been able to provide input, it does help build trust."

"Give credit to all partners whenever possible," advised Blair. "Give recognition whenever and however possible!"

MANAGING PARTNERSHIPS

At this point, you will want to consider how the partners should behave in the relationship. Obviously, cooperation is the ideal. But what should you do if another partner does not cooperate by fulfilling its commitments in a timely manner?

The work of actively managing partnerships can be supported by partnership norms, collaborative work plans, and solid communication structures and practices. We will explore each of these in this section.

Creating Partnership Norms

Relationships are the foundation of partnerships. Successful partnerships are managed by people who recognize the importance and benefit of cultivating healthy working relationships. In a large partnership comprised of many relationships, it becomes essential to establish parameters and guidelines on how partnership members will work together.

Creating and following partnership norms is an effective way to maintain healthy working relationships. *Partnership norms* are a set of shared values that act as informal guidelines on how partnership members will behave and interact with one another.

Creating partnership norms requires that you take the time to consider each person's past experience, work style, cultural values, expectations, and self-interest. In a collaborative environment, all these factors will surface and impact the ability of the group to effectively work together.

Many think that they create norms for their partnership when they sign a memorandum of understanding (MOU). While MOUs are formal agreements that establish the structure and roles and responsibilities of a partnership relationship, they do not establish the "how" of the relationship. MOUs are formal agreements between organizations, whereas partnership norms are informal standards for how individuals will work together.

You can develop partnership norms by implementing the following four steps:

1. **Identify the shared values of the group.**

   A partnership kickoff meeting is a good time to engage your partners in dialogue about establishing norms, often referred to as "ground rules." Discuss and identify the areas in which norms will be necessary. Suggested areas include communication, knowledge management, resource management, decision-making, conflict resolution, and/or meetings.

   Take time to listen to each person's perspective on each topic. Then, as a group, decide on what your shared values and norms will be. Partnership norms must be guidelines that are agreed upon by all members of the group.

2. **Document the partnership norms and make them easily accessible.**

   Based on your shared values, write statements that will serve as guidelines for behavior and how the group will work together. For example, if your partnership places a value on participant attendance at partnership meetings, suggested norms might read:

   - We will attend all partnership meetings regularly.

   - I will notify members in advance if I must miss a meeting.

   - I will ask another member of the group to debrief me within one week of missing any meetings.

   The use of "we will" or "I will" statements helps create ownership of the partnership norms. Once your norms are documented, make sure that they are easily accessible to everyone in the group. No matter how important or relevant information is, it is useless unless people are able to quickly access it. Consider posting your partnership norms on a shared website or virtual workspace.

3. **Communicate the partnership norms regularly.**

   People will have an opportunity to cultivate healthy working relationships the more visible the partnership norms are to them. Frequently communicating your partnership norms also emphasizes accountability to your shared values. Consider creating laminated cards or fact sheets that can be distributed to partnership members. You might also consider attaching a copy of partnership norms to all meeting notes.

4. **Update partnership norms as necessary.**

   Even if you maintain the same members throughout your partnership, it is necessary to revisit your norms and assess them based on the current developmental stage of your partnership. Staff turnover and organizational participation are factors in sustaining any partnership. As your partnership grows and it adds or loses members, it is important to revisit your partnership norms. Remember, partnership norms are only effective when all members of the group agree on the shared values.

Partnership Norms Template

An initial step in adopting partnership norms is to identify what your group values in collaborative working relationships. We have listed a few general areas and probing questions as examples.

WHERE CAN YOU ESTABLISH PARTNERSHIP NORMS?	WHAT ARE YOUR SHARED VALUES?	PARTNERSHIP NORM STATEMENTS
COMMUNICATION *Perspective-gathering questions:* » *What is important to you when you are talking to someone?* » *How do you communicate that you are looking for solutions versus looking for understanding?* » *What methods of communication work best for you? (email, phone, in person, etc.)*		
RESOURCE MANAGEMENT *Perspective-gathering questions:* » *What issues have you experienced in sharing your resources with others in collaborative partnerships (equipment and supplies, facilities, professional contacts, etc)?* » *What is an effective way for us to share our resources?*		
DECISION-MAKING *Perspective-gathering questions:* » *What has been your experience in collaborative decision-making? What do you find works best?* » *How do you like to be involved in solving collaborative issues?* » *When should a final decision be made (after we achieve complete consensus, after we have majority consensus, or after everyone has had the opportunity for feedback)?*		
CONFLICT RESOLUTION *Perspective-gathering questions:* » *How do you approach conflict in relationships?* » *What effective mediation strategies have worked for you?* » *How personally do you internalize work conflicts?*		

Designing Structures for Open, Honest Communication

Open, honest communication is a cornerstone of good partnerships and can be built by creating norms and structures for facilitated discussion. Successful partnerships use consistent communication norms in every interaction and meeting. They engage in open dialogue with parameters and include healthy conflict.

There are several methods for creating open, honest communication. A few methods include:

1. Hire a consultant to train all staff and partners on facilitation techniques.
2. Build proficiency in two or more leaders to develop understanding of at least one proven model of communication and commit to facilitating the model. Examples of proven models of communication include:

   - Fierce conversations

   - Difficult conversations

   - Crucial conversations

   - Crucial confrontations

3. Implement "leadership circles." An example is Women's Leadership Circles, a project of The Tides Center.

4. Participate in <u>Courage to Lead</u> workshops.
5. Provide executive/leadership coaching for all leaders within partner organizations to explore values and understand different perspectives.

The implementation steps for these methods vary depending on the method used. A few elements are consistent, independent of the method, including:

Facilitation

- The most essential element for this practice is a skillful facilitator and at least one alternate.
- Facilitators must be willing and able to uphold and model the principles/norms/ground rules/framework decided on.
- The facilitator must be adept at exposing inherent contradictions in systems and institutions.

Ground rules and norms

- Establish ground rules and norms for communication; create a framework to use for dialogue.
- All participants must agree to group norms and rules and be willing to hold each other accountable.
- Norms should be posted at each meeting.

Participants' needs and self-interest must be addressed. Why is each participant involved? What does each person hope to gain? What are they willing to commit? What would failure mean to their organization? What would a successful outcome look like?

The collaborative must learn how to engage in healthy, productive conflict. Conflict is necessary for facing contradictions that must be addressed for a collaborative to move forward and implement community-wide solutions.

Crafting Collaborative Work Plans

A collaborative work plan is a document that outlines the structure of work for the partnership or a specific initiative within the partnership. If your partnership is considering developing a collaborative work plan or is tracking progress on a work plan, keep in mind the following:

Establishing buy-in

Collaborative work plans document the work breakdown for your specific tasks—they cannot motivate people to action. Increase your success rate by first establishing buy-in from the members of your work group.

Being realistic

It is important to be realistic when developing a collaborative work plan. People want to see progress, no matter how incremental. Stay within the scope of your project.

Having measurable results

Consider developing short-term, intermediate, and long-term outcomes for your collaborative work plan. Identify how you will determine the success of your activities and efforts. What indicators will you measure?

Being accountable

Communicate group accountability and interdependence of activities. Showing people how their specific tasks impact the completion of the overall task is a good way of communicating the expectation of accountability. Having an effective structure for open, honest communication can support conversations of accountability as issues arise.

Collaborative Work Plan Worksheet

The following worksheet can be used to help develop a collaborative work plan. Some of these items will have been developed during Steps One and Two of partnership formation.

CONSIDERATIONS	SAMPLE STRATEGIES *These are illustrative but not exhaustive sample strategies. Adapt, add-to, or delete these sample strategies as you see fit for your partnership.*	WHAT STRATEGIES WILL YOU IMPLEMENT AND HOW WILL IT BE DONE?	STATUS
Establishing and Maintaining Buy-In	▪ Openly communicate the goals and objectives of the project. ▪ Understand each member's stake or interest in the partnership's success. ▪ Provide opportunities for people to give input on how the goals and objectives can be achieved. ▪ Provide opportunities for people give feedback on the proposed work activities and tasks prior to implementation. ▪ Continually communicate the progress to plan. ▪ Remind collaborative members about the big picture.		
Being Realistic	▪ Concentrate your efforts on a few specific areas that are explicitly linked to the partnership's aims and do not focus on too many broad issues. ▪ Regularly assess your deliverables, time frames, and allocated resources and revise as necessary. ▪ Distribute work equitably. ▪ Ask your peers to review the work plan and provide feedback on what is feasible given your resources.		
Having Measurable Results	▪ Identify at least one indicator of success for each specific task. ▪ Identify short, intermediate, and long-term outcomes you expect to achieve as a result of your collective work.		
Being Accountable	▪ Have specific due dates for tasks and goal completion. ▪ Clearly identify who is doing what. ▪ Regularly review and communicate progress to plan. ▪ Remind collaborative members about the big picture.		
Other			

Using Technology to Manage Your Partnerships

Partnership norms, communication practices, and collaborative work plans can all be supported and strengthened by the use of technology. There are a host of platforms that allow you to effectively collaborate with partners online. Here they are separated based on the depth of collaboration allowed by the system.

Methods for Distributing Information

These technologies are the least collaborative, as they simply allow a lead organization to distribute information across a network. They are perfect for times when you simply need to share a new resource, provide an alert about a deadline, or update your partners on the status of a project.

Electronic newsletters

Electronic newsletters are an effective method for sharing information to be read and used by your audience when it is most convenient for them. This is also the risk associated with electronic newsletters—recipients may never make the time to read them.

Websites

A partnership website can be created to provide information about the partnership's accomplishments and upcoming events, with links to each partner organization.

Electronic clearinghouses

An extension of the website model, an electronic clearinghouse is an online resource library. It is a database of searchable information that can be controlled and edited by a partner organization as a means for sharing multiple resources with a network of organizations.

Systems for Collaborating

If you want to go beyond information dissemination, consider using technology that allows multiple participants to have a voice. These platforms for communicating and sharing data allow partners to converse, edit a document together, and share data with each other.

Electronic mailing lists

An electronic mailing list, or listserv, allows all of the partners within a collaborative to have an online discussion via e-mail. When establishing the listserv, permission to post an e-mail can be granted to all partners, or the lead organization can serve as a "moderator" to check posts and allow permission before they can be viewed by other partners.

Shared documents

Google Docs provides free tools including a web-based calendar and a system for group sharing and editing of documents. A collaborative can establish a "shared drive" of documents on the web that all partners have access to, with any document edits being tracked. Project Spaces is another platform that allows users to share documents, as well as create electronic mailing lists.

Web-based databases

Web-based databases range in price, but the more customized you want it to be, the more it will cost. These databases can be a very effective means for multiple organizations to collect and track data, especially when customized to the specific needs of your collaborative.

Systems for Real-time Interaction

These technologies not only provide for online collaboration, but allow partners to work together online in real time, replicating as closely as possible the scenario of working in the same room.

Online chatting and internet forums

Online communication can be as informal as instant messaging (IM) or as formal as password-protected chat rooms. The latter approach requires a greater time commitment, so be strategic when choosing to implement it.

Online meetings and trainings

Online meetings and trainings are ideal when there is information that needs to be shared visually by several parties within a specific time frame. Much of the technology is free or reasonably priced, and there are several platforms to choose from, including Yugma, Zoho Meeting, ReadyTalk, GoToMeeting, and GoToWebinar.

Virtual workspaces

A virtual workspace enables you to conduct virtually all of your collaboration online, allowing partners to share information, share documents, and have a discussion in the same location. Google Sites allows partners to create a website together to announce events, keep a shared calendar, and host shared resources.

Systems for Managing the Project

Using web-based project management tools allows a lead organization to be completely transparent with project plans, roles and responsibilities, and deadlines.

Project management

Software such as Viewpath allows users to manage collaborative activities across dispersed partners. After the user inputs a Gantt chart of activities (a bar chart that illustrates a project schedule), the system can send reminders to partners based on their responsibilities and then provide team status updates in real time. The software can also provide the resources needed for a virtual workspace, with online communication capabilities and a holding place for shared documents.

Implementing Evaluation and Monitoring

All partnerships need to ensure that they have an ongoing program of monitoring and revising aims and objectives. This relates to the *performing* stage in team development. This should also provide the opportunity to learn what has been successful and what has not, building these lessons into revised plans.

You will want to build in performance management processes that facilitate monitoring and evaluation. The plan should set periodic reviews to check whether its aims and objectives have changed and what is required to make the change.

As the term of a partnership increases, the original vision and goals may become blurred. Existing partnership members may leave and new ones join. The following questions provide a useful tool by which new members will better understand what the partnership is about, as well as reinforce the partnership's original purpose and goals. Where there are negative responses to the following questions, the partnership needs to determine how it will take positive action to rectify the deficiencies.

QUESTIONS FOR EVALUATION AND MONITORING

Do partners share a common vision? Are partners willing to make changes to achieve shared goals?

Are the overall vision, purpose, and goals still recognized by members? Have these key definitions changed? If so, how was this communicated?

Notes:

What is the mandate of the partnership? Why was the group established, and are members still clear about this (benefits and added value)? Do members understand and agree to the purpose and accept it as important?

It is worth revisiting this to ensure members still understand the purpose of the partnership?

Notes:

Does the work of the group still link to overarching national/local policies and strategies?

If the work of the group does not easily fit or link into any such policies/strategies, ask why the group is in existence.

Notes:

Does the group possess shared values and accepted principles? If these are in place, has everyone agreed to them? Is everyone aware of these principles? Does the group still meet the original need for its existence?

Although these shared values and principles are mentioned throughout the process, you will want to revisit this whenever individuals leave the group and new members join. Also, government directives may change the focus of the group.

Notes:

Does the work of the group involve all relevant parties (i.e., users and carers)? If not, why not? Are users and the community involved in practice? If so, in what way?

Notes:

Has the group agreed upon a set of outcomes? Is everyone aware of these? How has the group measured progress against these outcomes? Is this done on a regular basis?

Notes:

Does the group work well together? How effectively does the group meet its aims and objectives? Do they agree on the aims and objectives? How are these reviewed and revised in light of any new policy/priorities?

Notes:

Is there a clear understanding of own/other's roles and responsibilities? Have these changed? How is this monitored?

Notes:

Is the purpose of the group known and understood outside the partnership itself? Is adequate information available about the partnership and its decisions? If there is a communication strategy, how effective has this been?

Notes:

Is there adequate monitoring, evaluation, and feedback? Does the partnership review its aims and objectives in the light of any changes/challenges to the outcomes?

Notes:

What do individuals/organizations expect to receive from the partnership? Has the partnership been successful in achieving its accepted outcomes? Is this communicated across the partnership/externally?

Notes:

Have any organizational improvements occurred after establishment of the partnership? What differences have resulted from the partnership?
Notes:
Is there mutual trust and respect? Are relationships between members good? If not, what action was taken to remedy this?
Notes:
Was the partnership supported by leaders/politicians (where relevant)? Were the aims/goals of the partnership clear to leaders/council members?
Notes:
Do formal and informal communications take place? Is there regular communication, or conflicting values/poor communication? Does the partnership work in an open or closed way?
Notes:
Does the membership of the partnership represent the right people? Does it fully represent target groups?
Notes:

KEY QUESTIONS FOR EVALUATION AND MONITORING

☐ Does the partnership still meet its aims and objectives?

☐ How well is it performing?

☐ What lessons can be learned?

PARTNERSHIP TRANSITION, ENDING, AND RENEWAL

Years after the Forming, Storming, Norming, and Performing Model was developed, its creator added an important final stage: *adjourning*. Every partnership must eventually consider issues of transition and ending. Some partnerships may use this time to renew goals and commitments. Others may find that it is time to let organizational partners go or end the partnership altogether.

Have an open and honest discussion with your partner(s) to understand when a coalition is transitioning into a stage of renewal or ending. Every partnership relationship is different. What motivates and engages each organization or individual to participate and to continue working collaboratively is different. Properly assessing your situation will help determine the best course of action. If people are bored or burned out ask, "Is the work of this group done? If not, then why are people feeling this way?"

In this stage, the primary question is, "Why continue?" Partnerships need closure. This step is often missed, as many partnerships either 1) end with a hard stop with no substantive communication between members or 2) end without an end—essentially dwindling down without closing out.

When you close a partnership, it's part of the natural cycle to consolidate learning. This is being done at an individual level, with or without the structured time. Among other concerns, partnership participants will be thinking individually about what worked, what didn't, who they learned from, and who they want to continue to learn from.

Since this is already happening at an individual level, you can capture that thinking and use it to help end in a way in which participants can any lessons learned with them onto their next activity or endeavor. Consolidating learning can happen through simple activities where members say what worked and what did not. It can also happen through individual and group reflections on lessons learned, accomplishments, and what needs to be left behind, or what is new and needs to be tackled now.

In some instances, it's one organization that wants to leave the partnership. In this case, you can discuss what would need to change to hold everyone's interest. Perhaps their disinterest is an early warning sign of others feeling the same way. In other situations, it may be in the best interest of not only the partner but also the collaborative as a whole that the relationship ends by allowing one group to leave on appropriate terms. Focusing all your time and resources on trying to convince a particular partner to stay can suggest that you don't value your current participating partners as highly. Ultimately, partnerships are effective when all members see a value in participating and willingly work together to achieve the common purpose.

APPENDICES

APPENDIX A

Resources/References

"Adams Elementary School Project Signals Forest Park Southeast's Rebirth." *Washington University Record*, October 27, 2000. http://wupa.wustl.edu/record_archive/2000/10-27-00/articles/adams.html.

Axelrod, Robert. "Conflict of Interest: An Axiomatic Approach." *Journal of Conflict Resolution* 11 (1967): 87-99.

Axelrod, Robert. *The Evolution of Cooperation*. New York, NY: Basic Books, 1985.

Axelrod, Robert. "On Six Advances in Cooperation Theory." *Analyse & Kritik* 22 (2000): 130-151.

Baum, Howell S. *The Organization of Hope: Communities Planning Themselves*. Albany, NY: State University of New York, 1997.

Boyer, Ernest L. *Scholarship Reconsidered: Priorities of the Professoriate*. Princeton, NJ: Carnegie Foundation for the Advancement of Teaching, 1997.

Chaskin, Robert J. *Defining Community Capacity: A Framework and Implications from a Comprehensive Community Initiative*. Chicago, IL: Chapin Hall Center for Children at the University of Chicago, 1999.

Chaskin, Robert J. *Defining Neighborhood: History, Theory, and Practice*. Chicago, IL: Chapin Hall Center for Children at the University of Chicago, 1995.

Chaskin, Robert J. and Prudence Brown. Theories of neighborhood change. In *Core Issues in Comprehensive Community-building Initiatives*. Rebecca Stone, ed. Chicago, IL: Chapin Hall Center for Children at the University of Chicago, 1996.

Chaskin, Robert J., Mark L. Joseph, and Selma Chipenda-Dansokho. *The Ford Foundation's Neighborhood and Family Initiative: The Challenge of Sustainability*. Chicago, IL: Chapin Hall Center for Children at the University of Chicago, 1997.

Chaskin, Robert J. and Clark Peters. *Decision Making and Action at the Neighborhood Level: An Exploration of Mechanisms and Processes*. Chicago, IL: Chapin Hall Center for Children at the University of Chicago, 2000.

Connolly, Paul and Peter York (2002). *Pulling Together: Strengthening the Nonprofit Sector through Strategic Restructuring*. New York, NY: TCC Group, 2002.

Eichler, Michael. "Consensus Organizing: Sharing Power to Gain Power." *National Civic Review* 84, no. 3 (2004): 256-262.

Essenburg, Timothy. "Urban Community Development: An Examination of the Perkins Model." *Review of Social Economy* 58, no. 2 (2000): 197-223.

Fulbright-Anderson, Karen, Patricia Auspos, and Andrea Anderson. *Community Involvement in Partnerships with Educational Institutions, Medical Centers, and Utility Companies*. Washington, DC: Aspen Institute, 2001.

Harkavy, Ira. "The Demands of the Times and the American Research University." *Journal of Planning Literature* 11, no. 3 (1997): 333-336.

Joseph, Mark and Renae Ogletree. "Community Organizing and Comprehensive Community Initiatives." *Journal of Sociology and Social Welfare* 25, no. 1 (1998):71–79.

Kilpatrick, Sue, Susan Johns, Bill Mulford, Ian Falk, and Libby Prescott. *More Than an Education: Leadership for Rural School-Community Partnerships.* Barton, ACT: Rural Industries Research and Development Corporation, 2002.

Lamb, Sara, Merwyn R. Greenlick, and Dennis McCarty, eds. *Bridging the Gap Between Practice and Research: Forging Partnerships with Community-based Drug and Alcohol Treatment.* Washington, DC: National Academy Press, 1998.

Mattessich, Paul W. and Barbara Monsey. *Community Building: What Makes It Work.* St. Paul: MN: Amherst H. Wilder Foundation, 1997.

McNeil, Ronald D. "Partners in the Marketplace: A New Model for Business-Civic Leadership." *National Civic Review* 84, no. 3 (1995): 248-255.

Sage, Linda. "HUD Grant Opens Doors to Forest Park Southeast Revitalization." *Washington University Record*, October 5, 1995. http://record.wustl.edu/archive/1995/10-05-95/6662.html.

Smith, Steven R. "Partnerships, Community Building, and Local Government." *National Civic Review* 86, no.2 (1997): 167-174.

Spruill, Nina, Con Kenney, and Laura Kaplan. "Community Development and Systems Thinking: Theory and Practice." *National Civic Review* 90, no. 1 (2001): 105-116.

Tranel, Mark and Kay Gasen. *Community Partnerships: A Sustainable Resource for Nongovernmental Organizations.* St. Louis, MO: UMSL Public Policy Research Center, 2003.

Walzer, Norman and Lori York. "Public-Private Partnerships in U.S. Cities," in *Public-Private Partnerships for Local Economic Development.* Norman Walzer and Brian D. Jacobs, eds. Westport, CT: Praeger Publishers, 1998.

Wright, David J. *Research Statement: A Study of Urban Neighborhoods and Community Capacity Building.* Albany, NY: Nelson A. Rockefeller Institute of Government, 1997.

APPENDIX B

Glossary

Advisory Partnership – Oversees specific plans, acting in an advisory capacity to ensure that strategies/ operational policies and plans are achieved.

Aims – What you intend to do/accomplish during the course of the partnership.

Business Plan – Sets out the operational and administrative aspects of the organization, as well as financial forecasts and supporting budgetary information. It will set out the broad developmental needs identified in a (long-term) strategy and specify how these needs will be assessed and met.

Contractual Partnership – Partners work together to jointly purchase/commission development on an operational basis.

Goals – The desired outcome; long-term, linking to targets.

Goals-based Coalition/Network Alliance – Partners work together to achieve agreed-upon goals, share information, and/or influence policy and strategy.

Intermediary – Something existing between two persons or things, or someone who acts as an agent or mediator between persons or things. An intermediary organization, then, exists between the people with the resources and the organizations needing the resources—namely finances or information.

Joint Venture Partnership – Partners work together to set up, implement, or manage.

Objectives – How you achieve your aims.

Principles – Fundamental rules, for example, on which services will be delivered. Standards should be based on outlined principles.

Project-based Partnership – Partners work together to monitor a specific project.

Quality – A degree of excellence. Approaches to quality should cover all customers/donors/providers, both internal and external.

Strategic Partnership – Partners work together to set out a specific joint strategy plan, with no specific operational role.

Strategy – Sets out the overall plan and direction. The development of strategic plans are phased elements in the planning processes.

Targets – The focus of short-term measures taken to achieve long-term goals.

Values – Beliefs, standards.

Vision – Concepts, hopes; why an organization wants to do something.

www.ingramcontent.com/pod-product-compliance
Lightning Source LLC
Chambersburg PA
CBHW080623180526
45168CB00007B/3039